Exploring Precalculus
with the
TI-89, TI-92, and TI-92PLUS

Michael B. Schneider
Belleville Area College

Lawrence G. Gilligan
College of Applied Science, University of Cincinnati

GILMAR Publishing
P.O. Box 6376
Cincinnati, OH 45206
(513) 751-8688

Printed in the United States of America

ISBN: 1-888808-04-7

This learning package (of text and files) is available in two formats:

1) Traditional text plus diskette of files
                        or
2) Totally electronically (download from http://www.mathware.com)

Cover design: Patricia Lloyd
Printing: United Graphics

The TI-89, TI-92, and TI-92 Plus Module are products of Texas
Instruments Incorporated. TI-Graph Link is a trademark of Texas
Instruments Incorporated.

GILMAR Publishing
P.O. Box 6376
Cincinnati, OH 45206
(513) 751-8688

CONTENTS

Preface

About the collection of files

There are over 35 files accompanying this text and they provide the basis for this project. These files are program and utility files, text files, data files, graphical data base files, and picture files. They are grouped into one large file which you will need to download to your calculator. If you have a TI-89, use the grouped file PRECALC.89g; if you have a TI-92PLUS, use the grouped file PRECALC.9xg; and if you have a TI-92, use the grouped file PRECALC.92g.

You will need a TI-Graph Link® cable and its accompanying software. (The software is downloadable from TI's website. The address from which you can select the appropriate file is http://www.ti.com/calc/docs/link.htm.)

You should make a new folder on your hard drive for the TI files you will use. Suppose you create a file called c:\precalc and you have a TI-89. Copy PRECALC.89g into that folder. Now run TI Graph Link 89 (be sure your cable is attached and the correct communications port is chosen in the Link menu). Click on "Link" then click on "Send."

Next, select the file PRECALC.89g; your screen should look

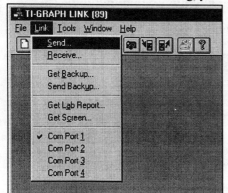 like the one to the right just before you click on "OK." The files should now be transferred to the main folder of your calculator. (Of course, if you have a TI-92 or TI-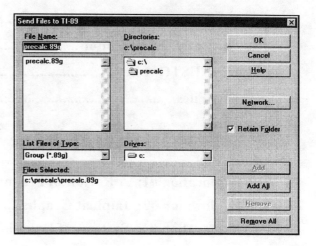

92PLUS, you will have to adjust these directions to use the correct filename extension.)

Acknowledgments

The cooperation of the people at Texas Instruments, Inc. has been invaluable. In particular, we are indebted to Michelle Miller, Scott L. Webb, Steve Reid, Yong Cui, Gosia Brothers for their encouragement and support.

Jerry and Joyce Glynn of MathWare, Ltd are long time friends and innovators in learning. Their involvement in making this book available in a totally electronic format made it happen and we are excited to be part of their innovation.

As always, thanks to Patricia Lloyd for her talents on the cover design.

Finally but foremost, we are indebted to our families for their love, support and understanding as we emailed, programmed, wrote, and rewrote. It is for them that we dedicate this book.

An Overview of the TI-89, TI-92 and TI-92PLUS

The MODE Key

There are three pages (two pages on the TI-92) of choices for the mode settings which control how algebraic expressions, numbers, matrices and graphs are displayed and interpreted. The three pages along with the default settings are shown below:

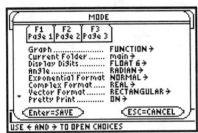 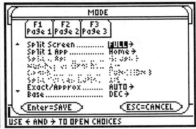 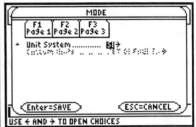

To change a setting, simply cursor down to it and press the right cursor key to choose from a list of options for that particular item.

For example, to split the screen into two parts vertically, on page 2[1] we change the settings to:

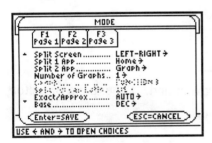

Left: Choose "LEFT-RIGHT" for the screen split. We also chose the left-hand split ("Split 1 App") to be the home screen and the right side split to be the graph window.

Right: The home screen is on the left and the graph screen on the right. (We graphed a function

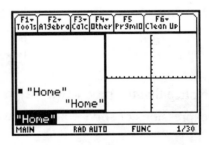

To see how the mode settings can affect the appearance of numerical results, we will return the screen to "FULL" and display the output of the calculation $\frac{1}{8} + \frac{4}{7}$ three ways.

TIPS!
1. Always stay in "AUTO" mode.
2. When you press the ENTER key, you will get an exact answer, if the calculator is capable of finding it. When you press the ◆ ENTER keys, you will get an *approximate* answer!

First, we enter the fraction and press the ENTER key to see the exact result. Next, change the "Display Digits" setting to "E:FLOAT" and, upon returning to the HOME screen, press ◆ ENTER to approximate the result. For a third setting, try "4:FIX 3" as the choice for the display. We depict all three in the screen capture below:

---

[1] Reach page 2 by pressing F2 after pressing the MODE key

In "FLOAT" mode, $\frac{1}{8}+\frac{4}{7}$ is displayed as .696428571429; in "FIX 3" mode, it is .696.

Another TIP!

When there are lots of items in a list from which to choose (such as the 25 alternatives in the "Display Digits" menu), select an item by pressing its first character code. To choose "E:FLOAT" for example, press ALPHA E. It is not necessary to cursor down to your choice.

Algebra on the HOME Screen

The power of these calculators is their ability to do symbolic manipulation. Expressions will be simplified, if possible, when entered and we show a screen below with several algebraic entries.

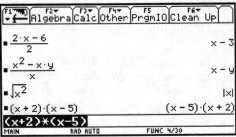

Notice that the product $(x+2)(x-5)$ does not automatically get expanded. To expand or factor expressions or solve equations, we invoke the "F2 Algebra" menu.

Another TIP!

To clear the home screen, press F1 and then choose "8:Clear home". Press the CLEAR key to clear all entries to the right of the cursor on the edit line. (If the cursor is all the way to the right, the entire line is cleared.)

There are eleven options under the "Algebra" menu. Notice how factor and cfactor (for factoring over the complex numbers) differ.

There is a lot of versatility in the algebra commands. "Solve(" for example can be used to solve an equation for a specific variable. "Expand(" can be used to write a fraction as a sum of two or more fractions (called *partial fraction decomposition*) and "Zeros(" returns a list of zeros of an expression. See the screen below for specific examples.

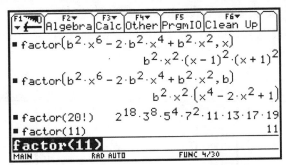

Some additional algebra command examples.

The factor command can yield different results depending upon the variable you want to factor with respect to. The first two lines of the screen below differ only by first factoring with respect to x and then with respect to b. The other two lines are there to show you can factor numbers, too. (If the number is returned, it is a prime number.)

The factor command examples screen.

More Tips!

1. Beware of implicit multiplication! While $2x$ is understood to mean 2 times x, the expression xy represents a single variable with a two-letter name. To enter $x*y$ you need to use the multiplication key.
2. After a while, you may want to use letters that have been previously assigned. The convenient [F6] key clears out single letter variable names.
3. The previous line's output can be accessed without retyping it – simply press [2nd][ANS]!

There are other algebra commands. "comDenom(" will return a reduced fraction with one numerator and one denominator. "propFrac(" returns a proper fraction and "cZeros(" returns a list of complex zeros for an expression.

The screen below illustrates these commands.

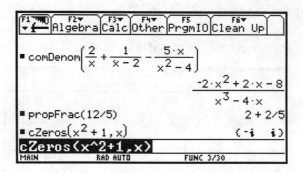

The reader is urged to experiment with these commands as well as those not listed here.

Graphing

To graph functions of a single independent variable involves getting familiar with the Y= editor, the WINDOW editor, and the graph window. These are labeled in green (in conjunction with the ◆ key). The first function we will graph is $f(x) = (x+2)(x-1)^2$. To enter it, enter the Y= editor, press ENTER and type in the expression $(x+2)*(x-1)^2$.

Now enter the WINDOW editor and set the values to their default settings by pressing F2 and then choose "6:ZoomStd".

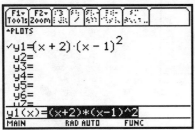
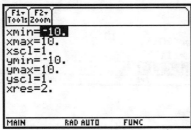
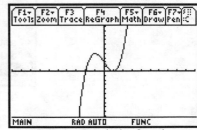

| Step 1: Enter the function. | Step 2: Choose WINDOW values. | Step 3: Graph the function. |

Before graphing additional functions or examining different window settings, we mention here that the graph screen can be formatted for different appearances. To see the format options, press F1 and choose "9:Format." You should see these possible format options:

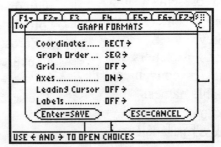

To add a grid, for example, select "Grid" and choose "ON." After pressing ENTER to save the change, revisit the graph screen. You should see a graph paper-like grid.

In addition to formatting options, you can also select the style of the graph. This is done from the Y= editor. With the function to be styled highlighted, press F6. Choose "4:Thick" and observe the graph now. We show it below with the grid on:

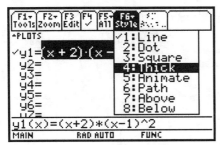 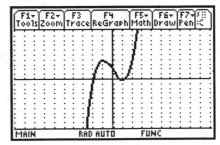

The graph of $f(x) = (x+2)(x-1)^2$ with a thick style and "Grid" turned on.

By the way, now that the function $f(x) = (x+2)(x-1)^2$ is defined in the Y= editor, it can be used from other areas of the calculator. For example, we could find the function's zeros from the HOME screen or even evaluate $f(2)$. You have to use its designation, $y1(x)$, however, in either case. We perform those two operations below:

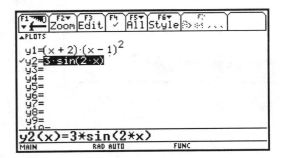

We now present a second graphing example, $f(x) = 3\sin(2x)$. It is entered as $y2(x)$ in the Y= editor. To be sure we *only* see the graph of $y2(x) = 3\sin(2x)$, we "uncheck" $y1(x)$ by pressing F4 when $y1$ is highlighted.

Next, we decide to split the screen vertically in a 1:1 ratio. Also, there is a built in ZoomTrig collection of WINDOW settings. This is obtained by pressing F2 (for the Zoom menu) and then "7:ZoomTrig" from the Y= editor, the WINDOW editor, or the graph screen.

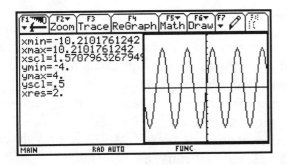

Another TIP!
On a split screen, the 2nd APPS key toggles from one of the split screens to the other. Its icon is ⊞.

An interesting challenge is to approximate graphically the solutions of the equation $(x+2)(x-1)^2 = 3\sin(2x)$ or, in the language of the calculator, solve $y1(x) = y2(x)$ for x. To do this, we re-select $y1(x)$ and examine the graph of both functions. Next, we invoke the F5 Math menu and select "5:Intersection" from the list. Since there are three intersections, we will only find one here, the only negative solution. See the screens below:

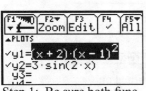 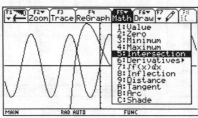 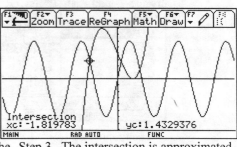

Step 1: Be sure both functions are selected (F4).

$$(x+2)(x-1)^2 = 3\sin(2x)$$

Step 2: Choose :5:Intersection from the F5 menu. You will then be prompted to indicate the functions and then a lower bound and an upper bound for the point of intersection.

Step 3. The intersection is approximated. A solution to

is $x \approx -1.819783$

Alternatively, we could have solved for x on the HOME screen.

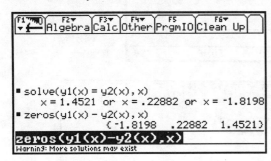

The reader should realize that the following three statements are equivalent:

1. The value x is the abscissa of the point of intersection of the graphs of $y = y1(x)$ and $y = y2(x)$.

2. The value x is the solution to the equation $y1(x) = y2(x)$.

3. The value x is a zero of the expression $y1(x) - y2(x)$.

Additional Editing TIPS!

1. The backspace key, ←, deletes the character to the *left* of the cursor. Often, ◆ ← is more convenient – it deletes the character to the *right* of the cursor.

2. Instead of searching various menus for a particular function or command, it may be easier to use the [CATALOG]. Once it is selected, press the first letter of the command to index to that portion of the catalog.

3. If an item in a pull-down menu has a ▶ to its right, then that item has a submenu.

4. To recall a previous entry, press [2nd][ENTRY]. Press it twice to recall the second past entry, etc.

Tables

To display a table of numerical values that represent points on graphs, we begin by setting up the table parameters by pressing ◆[TblSet] . Two important values have to be put into the table: a starting *x* value (labeled tblStart) and an *x*-increment (labeled as Δtbl). In the Y= editor, we will be sure $y1(x)$ and $y2(x)$ are both selected. Next, we choose to start the table at $x = -5$ and increment the *x* values by 0.5. We display the table setup screen and the table of values below:

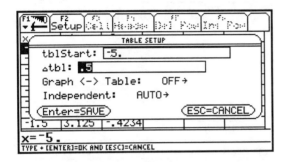

A popular option is to set the Graph <-> Table switch to "ON" so that then the *x* values correspond to pixel breaks on the graph (the values that get traced). We depict that option in a split screen so the table and the graphs are visible.

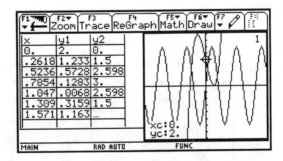

Additional Graphing TIPS!

1. To stop a function from being graphed, press the [ON] key.
2. To pause a function while it is being graphed, press the [ENTER] key; Press it again to resume graphing.

The Data/Matrix Editor

The Data/Matrix editor is used to enter and operate on lists, matrices, and sets of data. We begin by examining the data of five milestone closings of the Dow Jones Industrial Average

(DJIA). To enter the data below, press the APPS key and choose item "6:Data/Matrix Editor." Then select "3:New" and give the data set the name DJIA

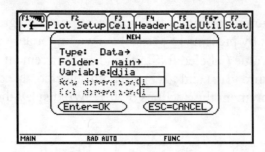

The data is given below"

Date	Coded Date	DJIA
	(in years since 1/1/1906)	
	x values entered in $c1$	Y values entered in $c2$
Nov. 14, 1972	66.9	1003
Jan. 8, 1987	81.1	2002
April 7, 1991	85.3	3004
Feb. 23, 1995	89.2	4003
Nov. 21, 1995	89.9	5000

The date information is placed into column c1 and the DJIA is in c2. It is optional to label the columns at the very top cell. We show the entered data below:

Is the data linear? quadratic? exponential? The best way to answer that question is to examine a plot of the data. To do this, we choose F2 for Plot Setup, then F1 to define Plot #1. See the screen below:

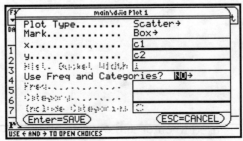

We examine a plot of the data but first, we adjust the WINDOW values.

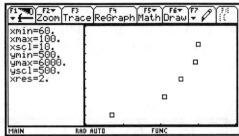

It appears the data is exponential. If you re-enter the data screen (APPS, "6:Data/Matrix Editor", "1:Current") and type F5 to calculate, we can find an exponential equation of best fit. See how we selected the parameters in the screen below:

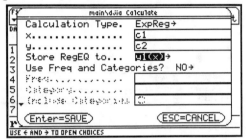

Notice that we have decided to store the equation in $y1(x)$.

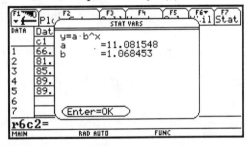

Finally, the exponential regression function, $y1(x) = 11.081548 \cdot 1.068453^x$ is graphed along with the scatter plot of the data in the screen below:

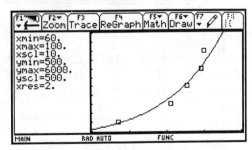

The CUSTOM key

Sometimes it is difficult to find a particular command or inconvenient to type it. For that reason, we can add a customized menu system for those often used or hard-to-find commands or symbols.

We have provided the program cust1() which will give you an idea as to how to write a program that will access the 2nd CUSTOM key. To use the features of this program, two steps must be followed: First, run the program by entering cust1() on the HOME screen and then press ENTER key. Second, press the 2nd CUSTOM keys. You should see a new menu system as displayed below:

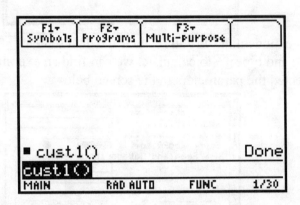

This program creates three pull down menus labeled "Symbols," "Programs," and "Multi-purpose." If you press the 2nd CUSTOM keys again, the default menu system is redisplayed.

To see how this can be used as a convenience, we have the program "partfrac" as the sixth item in "F2 Programs." To find the partial fraction decomposition of $\dfrac{x}{x^2-4}$, for example, we first store $\dfrac{x}{x^2-4}$ in the variable named "fraction". Then simply press the F2 key followed by the 6 key to obtain:

Text Files

We conclude this *Overview* by mentioning that it is sometimes convenient to save work done on the home screen or to create a series of important definitions or other commands. This can be done by saving a home screen in a text file or creating a new text file in the text editor (from the APPS key). This latter concept is sometimes referred to as *scripting.*

We have included two dual-purpose text files. They are called TOURALG and TOURTRIG. The first purpose of each is to walk the user through the various commands. We can examine the TOURALG text by pressing the [APPS] key, choosing "9:Text Editor" and then "2:Open." Type the name touralg and press the [ENTER] key twice.

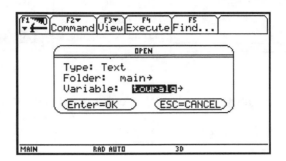

The file has many lines where each line is either a remark or a command. Commands are executable and are denoted with a leading "C" on the line. Remarks, of course, are not executable. While it is intended to use these from the top to the end, we will show the effect of executing a few lines.

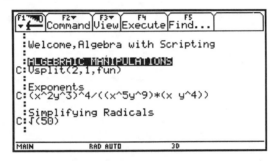

Scroll the cursor down to the line command line under the remark "Simplifying Radicals" where the command is $\sqrt{(50)}$. Press the [F4] key to execute this command and notice that the command is pasted into the HOME screen edit line and executed. It happens so fast, and your are returned to the text editor, that you barely notice anything. Move the cursor down to the next command line, approx($\sqrt{(50)}$) and press the [F4] key again. Now return to the HOME screen to see the two executed statements.

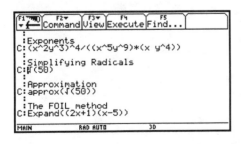

Left: The text editor displays several lines from the text file, TOURALG.

Right: Two command lines were executed and displayed on the HOME screen.

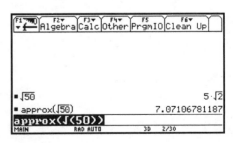

We conclude this section by showing some results of executing commands from the text file called TOURTRIG.

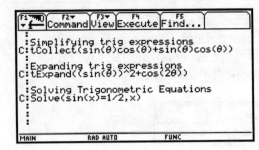

The three commands at the left are executed, one by one.

The results are seen on the home screen at the right.

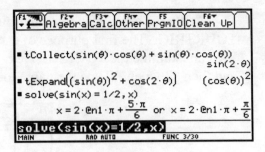

The final line of output (for the solve command) is curious. The symbol @n1 stands for an arbitrary integer. So, $2 \cdot @n1 \cdot \pi + \dfrac{5\pi}{6}$ really means $\dfrac{5\pi}{6}$ plus any integer multiple of 2π.

Exploration #1
A Review of Preliminaries

The program alg() creates a customized menu of five subprogram items. They are "$\boxed{F1}$ Dist" (to find the distance between two points), "$\boxed{F2}$ Slope" (to calculate the slope of the line through two given points), "$\boxed{F3}$ Quad" (to find the solutions to a quadratic equation), "$\boxed{F4}$ m,pt" (to compute the equation of a straight line given its slope and a point on the line), and "$\boxed{F5}$ Quit" to exit the program alg().

Example 1. The Distance Formula. Find the distance between the two points $(3,\ 6)$ and $(-2,\ -6)$.

Solution: After running alg(), we choose $\boxed{F1}$ and enter the four coordinates:

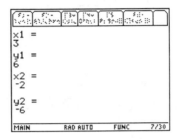

The distance is output as 13 units.

Example 2. Point-Slope Form. Using the same two points, $(3,\ 6)$ and $(-2,\ -6)$, find the slope of the line passing through them and the equation of that line.

Solution: It is very straightforward; we will use the $\boxed{F2}$ menu option of alg() to find slope and the $\boxed{F4}$ menu option to find the line's equation. When we use $\boxed{F2}$, we find the value of the slope is $m = \frac{12}{5}$. Now, we display the screens for finding the line's equation below. (We chose the point (3, 6) as (x0,y0).)

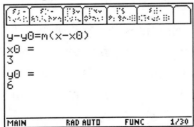

The equation of the line is $y = \frac{12}{5}x - \frac{6}{5}$

■

Example 3. The quadratic formula. Use alg() to solve the quadratic equation
$2x^2 + 5x - 3 = 0$.

Solution: The program walks you through the input of the three coefficients.

```
ax²+bx+c=0
a =
2
b =
5
c =
-3
1st root:
-3
2nd root:
1/2
MAIN        RAD AUTO      FUNC      PAUSE
```

The two solutions are $x = -3$ and $x = \frac{1}{2}$.

■

A general note: If you see the **PAUSE** indicator in the bottom right-hand corner, it means that to continue, you should hit the [ENTER] key. Also, to return to the HOME screen from the I/O screen, press the [F5] key.

Problems:

1. Find the distance between the points (2, 3) and (4, 5)

2. Find the distance between the points (-2, -3) and (-4, -5).

3. Find the slope of the line which passes through the points (2, 1) and (5, 7).

4. Find the equation of the line which passes through the points (2, 1) and (5, 7).

5. Find the equation of the line which passes through the point (1, 5) and is parallel to the line in question number 4. (Recall that parallel lines have equal slopes.)

6. Find the equation of the line which passes through the point (1, 1) and is perpendicular to the line in question number 5. (Recall that perpendicular lines have the property that the product of their slopes is −1.)

7. a) Choose any point on the line $y = 3x - 4$ and find the equation of the line perpendicular to $y = 3x - 4$ passing through your chosen point.
   b) Find the point of intersection of the line found in part a) and the line $y = 3x - 2$.
   c) Find the distance between your chosen point and the point found in part b). What does this distance represent?

8. When water boils it is measured as either 100 degrees Celsius or 212 degrees Fahrenheit. It freezes at either 0 degrees Celsius or 32 degrees Fahrenheit. Find the equation of the line that passes through (100, 212) and (0, 32). What have you found?

9. Solve: $4x^2 = 4x - 1$

10. An object is thrown upward from the top of a 160-ft high building with an initial speed of 80 ft/sec. The formula that represents its height h (in feet) after t seconds have elapsed is $h = -16t^2 + 80t + 160$. When will the object hit the ground?

11. A square piece of cardboard is to be formed into an open-top box by cutting 2 cm squares out of each corner and folding up the sides. If the volume of the box is to be 968 cm^3, what should the dimensions of the cardboard be?

Mathematical Background: This exploration reviews some topics from previous courses including *the distance formula*, the notion of *slope*, the *point-slope form* of a straight line, and solving quadratic equations using the *quadratic formula*. Given the two points (x_1, y_1) and (x_2, y_2):[2]

    1) The distance between them is given by $\sqrt{(x_1 - x_2)^2 + (y_1 - y_2)^2}$.

    2) The slope of the line passing through them is $m = \frac{y_2 - y_1}{x_2 - x_1}$

    3) The equation of the line passing through them is $y = m(x - x_1) + y_1$

The general quadratic equation is given by $ax^2 + bx + c = 0$, where $a \neq 0$. The two solutions are $x = \dfrac{-b + \sqrt{b^2 - 4ac}}{2a}$ and $x = \dfrac{-b - \sqrt{b^2 - 4ac}}{2a}$.

Program syntax: The program alg() is menu driven and allows the user to choose from four categories. It takes no parameters.

---

[2] We assume here that $x_1 \neq x_2$. If $x_1 = x_2$, then the slope is *undefined*, the line is vertical and its equation is given by $x = x_1$.

Exploration #2

Implicit Graphs

Example 1 Graph the hyperbola $x^2 - y^2 = 9$ for $-4 \le x \le 4$ and $-4 \le y \le 4$.

Solution: We manually set the graphing window before we call the program
implicit(). See the screen below for our choices:

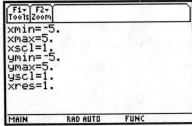

The program is invoked by entering implicit($x^2 - y^2 = 9$, $-4,4$).

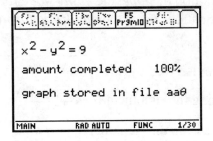

The output is displayed below.

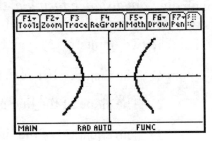

Notice that picture is stored in a file named *aaθ*. This picture file can be
viewed at a later date from the Graph screen by choosing "1:Open" from the
F1 Tools menu.

We conclude this example by mentioning that the program executes a
ZoomSqr operation so the window values will be adjusted to insure proper
perspective. For the hyperbola graphed above, for example, the resulting
window values on a TI-89 were:

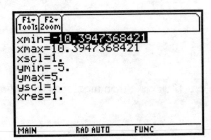

The graph in Example 1 could have been done as a graph of the two functions $y1(x) = \sqrt{x^2 - 9}$ and $y2(x) = -\sqrt{x^2 - 9}$ because in this case it is possible to solve $x^2 - y^2 = 9$ for y in terms of x. In Example 2, we present a relation that cannot be solved for y in terms of x.

Example 2 Graph $x^5 - x^2y^3 = xy$.

Solution: A word of caution: the term xy must be entered as the multiplication of x with y, that is $x*y$. The graph appears below:

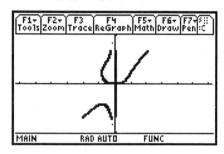

Problems.
1. Show that the y-axis is part of the solution to the graph in Example 2.
2. Sketch $y^2 + xy = 9$ and select your own bounds.
3. Sketch the graph of $x^{2/3} + y^{2/3} = 1$.

The equations listed for questions 4 through 7 are each a ***conic section***. Sketch the graph of each with an appropriate choice of bounds.

4. $34x^2 - 24xy + 41y^2 = 25$ 5. $34x^2 - 185xy + 41y^2 = 25$

6. $9x^2 - 24xy + 16y^2 - 80x - 60y + 100 = 0$ 7. $\sqrt{2}x^2 - 2\sqrt{2}xy + \sqrt{2}y^2 - 4x - 4y = 0$

8. We point out that there is another way to plot two-dimensional implicit relations but it only works on the TI-89 and TI-92PLUS (not the TI-92). To plot $x^2 - y^2 = 9$, for example, we think of it as $z = x^2 - y^2 - 9$. Set the graph mode to "3D" and enter $x^2 - y^2 - 9$ as $z1$. Then, under the format option, the style needs to be set to "IMPLICIT."

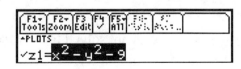
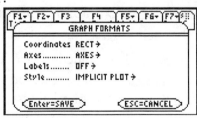

A set of window values and the graph appear below. Keep in mind that since this is a 3-D plot, we can spin the graph to gain perspectives from different viewpoints.

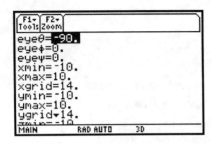 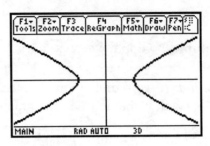

Use this approach to graph the ellipse $x^2 + 2y^2 = 12$.

9. In this exercise we show an alternative to plotting the relation in example 1. Recall, we mentioned that the equation $x^2 - y^2 = 9$ can be solved for y in terms of x – yielding two functions, $y1(x) = \sqrt{x^2 - 9}$ and $y2(x) = -\sqrt{x^2 - 9}$. We graph them below.

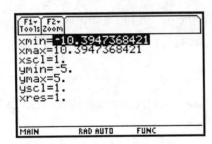 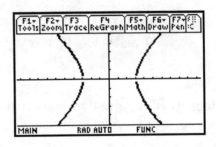

Notice the gap near the x axis. This often occurs and is one reason why we prefer to use the program implicit even for conic sections. Regraph $y1(x) = \sqrt{x^2 - 9}$ and $y2(x) = -\sqrt{x^2 - 9}$ after doing a ZoomDec. The gap disappears. Why?

Mathematical Background: This is a *utility* for plotting relations that are expressed implicitly. Recall, a function like $f(x) = x^2 - 9$, for example, is said to be ***explicitly*** expressed as a function of x. The relation $x^2 + y^2 = 9$ is not solved for one variable in terms of the other method and is an example of an implicit relation.

Program Syntax: The implicit program requires three arguments: the equation, a lower bound for both the domain and range and an upper bound for the domain and range:
implicit(relation, lowerbound, upperbound)
Also, this program calls another program called bigdot(). Be sure bigdot() is in the same folder as implicit().

Systems of Equations in Two Variables

Example 1   Solve the system of two linear equations in two variables:

$$4x - y = 5$$

$$8x - 3y = 13$$

Solution: We demonstrate four methods for solving this ***linear system***. The simult command is useful for solving a system of n linear equations in n variables provided the system has a unique solution. The coefficient matrix is entered in variable m1 and the constants are entered in matrix m2. Then we call simult(m1,m2) to solve the system.

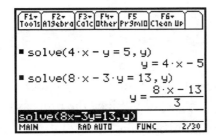

A second approach is to solve the system graphically – which is especially handy if there is not a unique solution to a system. Of course, we must first solve each equation for y. The "5:Intersection" option of F5 Math in the Graph screen verifies our answer that $x = \dfrac{1}{2}$ and $y = -3$.

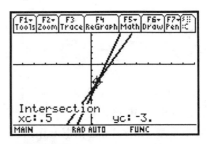

The third way of solving this system is to employ the solve command.[3] The variation we need is shown below. The equations are entered separated by the word "and" and then followed by a list of the variables:

---

[3] This option is only available on the TI-89 and TI-92PLUS. For TI-92 users, one of the other three methods will have to suffice.

Finally, we can use the program sys() to solve the system. By entering sys($\{4x - y = 5, 8x - 3y = 13\}$) we obtain a screen with seven options (controlled by the function keys):[4]

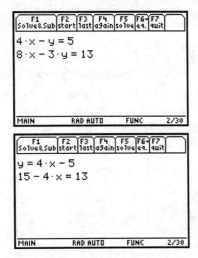

Left: The two equations appear.

Right: Choose [F1] then solve for y in equation one.

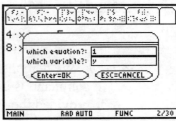

Left: The result of solving equation 1 for y and substituting that in equation 2.

Right: Now choose to solve for x in equation 2.

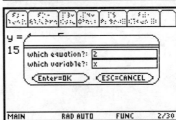

After pressing the enter key, the solution is determined and output. See the screen below.

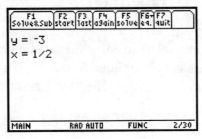

Example 2   Solve the non-linear system
$$2x - y = 1$$
$$y = 9 - x^2$$

Solution: We choose to employ the solve() command. By entering

solve($2x - y = 1$ and $y = 9 - x^2, \{x, y\}$). Since the process is identical to what was done in Example 1, we show only the final solution screen below:

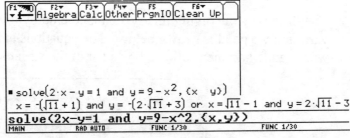

---

[4] Your screen displays may differ slightly. The TI-92 gives equivalent equations but with a slightly different appearance.

In other words, the solutions are: $x = -\sqrt{11} - 1 \approx -4.32, y = -2\sqrt{11} - 3 \approx -9.63$ and $x = \sqrt{11} - 1 \approx 2.32$, $y = 2\sqrt{11} - 3 \approx 3.63$. A graphical substantiation is presented below:

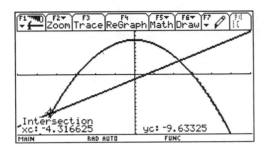 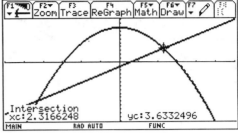

If we use sys() to solve this system, we obtain the screens below:

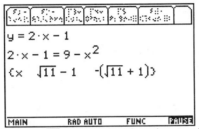

Left: After choosing F1 and solving for y in equation 1, then choose F5 and solve for x in equation 2..
Right: Select F1 and solve equation 1 for x and then choose F5 to solve for y in equation 2. ∎

Finally, we mention that the program sys2() (which will only run on the TI-89 or TI-92Plus) displays the solutions in pairs. For the system of Example 2, we enter the following: $\text{sys2}\left(\left\{2x - y = 1, y = 9 - x^2\right\}, \left\{x, y\right\}\right)$ and observe the two screens of output shown below.

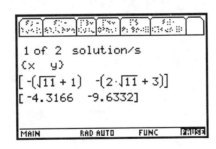 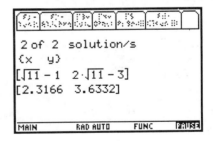

Problems:

Solve the system of equations in questions 1 through 4.

1.
$$x + y = 14$$
$$2x - y = -26$$

2.
$$2x + 3y = 4$$
$$4x + 5y = 6$$

3. $\begin{aligned} x_2 &= 2x_1 - 1 \\ 2x_1 + x_2 &= 9 \end{aligned}$

4. $\begin{aligned} s + t &= -3 \\ 2s - t &= 0 \end{aligned}$

A system of linear equations that has no solution is called an ***inconsistent system***; a system with infinitely many solutions is called a ***dependent system.*** Use a graphical approach to determine whether the systems in questions 5 and 6 have a unique solution, are independent or inconsistent.

5. $\begin{aligned} y &= \frac{1}{2}x - 2 \\ 3x - 4y &= 8 \end{aligned}$

6. $\begin{aligned} 2x + 3y &= 4 \\ 4x + 5y &= 6 \end{aligned}$

7. A company has two cost concerns: material (measured in tons) and labor (measured in hours). January'' total cost was $2500 involving 3 tons of material and 100 hours of labor. February's total cost was $3500 involving 4 tons of material and 150 hours of labor. Find the cost of one ton of material and one hour of labor.

8. The length of a rectangle is 5 meters more than its width. The perimeter is 24 meters. What are the dimensions of the rectangle?

9. Janet invested a total of $1000 in two stocks – one that yielded a 5% profit after a year and one that yielded a 6% annual profit. If she made $54 last year, how much was invested in each stock?

In questions 10 through 15, solve each nonlinear system. In each case, graph the system as a check. For some questions, the program implicit() may be useful (see Exploration #2).

10. $\begin{aligned} y &= x^2 - x - 12 \\ y &= x - 4 \end{aligned}$

11. $\begin{aligned} x^2 + y^2 &= 36 \\ x^2 - y^2 &= 36 \end{aligned}$

12. $\begin{aligned} x^2 + y^2 &= 9 \\ \frac{x^2}{9} - \frac{y^2}{4} &= 1 \end{aligned}$

13. $\begin{aligned} xy + 6 &= 0 \\ 3x + y &= 7 \end{aligned}$

14. $\begin{aligned} y &= \frac{4}{x} \\ x + y &= 5 \end{aligned}$

15. $\begin{aligned} x^2 + y^2 &= 20 \\ x^2 - y^2 &= 12 \end{aligned}$

16. The hypotenuse of a right triangle is 8.2 meters long and the area of the triangle is 7.2 square meters. Find the lengths of the two legs of the triangle.

Mathematical Background: In this exploration we examine several examples of solving a collection of equations in two variables. In a later exploration, we will extend this to systems of equations in many variables.

Here, we will assume all equations involve just two variables, x and y. Such an equation is called *a linear equation* if it is of the form $ax + by = c$ where a, b, and c are constants. Recall, a system of linear equations may have a unique solution (in two-space, intersecting lines), no solution (in two-space, parallel lines), or infinitely many solutions (in two-space, concurrent lines).

The systems we will explore involve both linear and nonlinear equations.

Program syntax: This exploration offers the option of using the program sys(). Sys() takes as its argument a list of equations. Thus, its syntax looks like:

$$sys(\{eqn1, eqn2, ...\})$$

We also introduce the program sys2() which takes both a list of equations and a list of variables as its argument:

$$Sys2(\{eqn1, eqn2, ...\}, \{var1, var2, ...\})$$

Exploration #4
Area of Triangles

Program syntax: The program triarea() takes no parameters and the following popup menu appears upon running it:

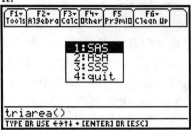

Example 1   In triangle ABC suppose the sides are given as $a = 6$, $b = 4$, and $c = 5$. Find the area.

Solution: This is an SSS situation and upon choosing that option, a dialog box appears. We enter the lengths of the three sides. See the figure below.

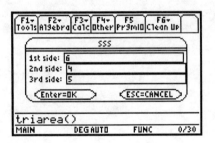

We see that the area is approximately 9.92 square units.

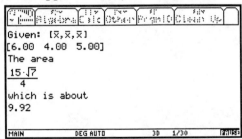

Example 2   Find the area of the triangle with parts: $a = 6.9$ cm, $b = 9.4$ cm, and $\angle C = 58°$

Solution: This is the SAS case and the reader is urged to try to draw a triangle accurately with these dimensions

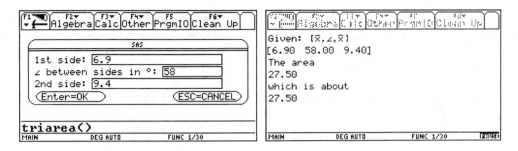

The area is 27.5 cm^2.

Problems:

For each of the questions 1-6 below, assume the upper case letters are the angles of a triangle and their lower case versions are the sides opposite them. Find the area, if possible, of the triangle with the given parts. If the area is not possible to determine, state why.

1.　　$a = 18$, $b = 14$, and $c = 10$.

2.　　$a = 6$, $b = 14$, and $c = 10$.

3.　　$A = 23°$, $b = 14$, and $C = 48°$.

4.　　$A = 73°$, $b = 54$, and $C = 4°$.

5.　　$a = 6$, $B = 14°$, and $c = 10$.

6.　　$b = 23.4$, $C = 34°$, and $a = 30$.

7.　In triangle ABC below, perform the following steps:

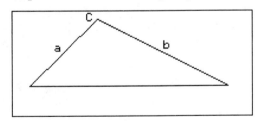

a)　Drop a perpendicular from angle C to the side AB. Label that height h and label the point where the perpendicular meets AB as point D.

b)　Show that in triangle BCD, $h = a \cdot \sin B$ and that in triangle ACD, $h = b \cdot \sin A$.

c)　Since the area of triangle ABC is $\dfrac{1}{2} base \cdot height$, show that that area could be expressed as $\dfrac{1}{2} a \cdot c \cdot \sin B$.

Mathematical Background: There are several formulas for finding the area of a triangle. $A = \frac{1}{2}bh$ is useful, for example, if you know the length of one side ("base") as well as the height (h). **Heron's formula**, $A = \sqrt{s(s-a)(s-b)(s-c)}$, is useful if you know the length of all three sides (a, b, and c) where s is the semi-perimeter ($s = \frac{a+b+c}{2}$) of the triangle.

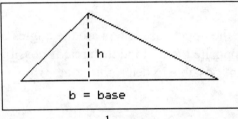 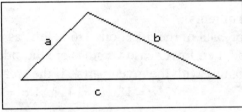

Left: $A = \frac{1}{2}bh$ Right: $A = \sqrt{s(s-a)(s-b)(s-c)}$ where $s = \frac{a+b+c}{2}$

Also, the area of a triangle is equal to one half the product of any two sides times the sine of the angle between them:

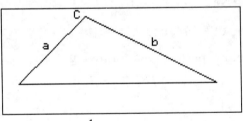

$$A = \frac{1}{2} \cdot a \cdot b \cdot \sin C$$

Exploration #5
Circles

Example 1   Show that $x^2 + y^2 - 4x + 8y + 11 = 0$ is the equation of a circle and find its center and radius. What are the domain and range of this relation?

> *Solution:* The equation $x^2 + y^2 - 4x + 8y + 11 = 0$ indeed does represent a circle because after completing the square, it becomes $(x - 2)^2 + (y + 4)^2 = 9$. After we run the program centcir($x^2 + y^2 - 4x + 8y + 11 = 0$) we observe the following output:

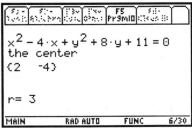

Using the utility *implicit()*, we see a sketch:

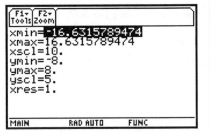 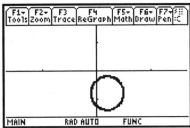

> The domain of any circle of the form $(x - h)^2 + (y - k)^2 = r^2$ is $h - r \le x \le h + r$ and its range is $k - r \le y \le k + r$. So for this example, the domain is $-1 \le x \le 5$ and the range is $-7 \le y \le -1$

Problems:

For each of the questions 1 through 4 below: a) determine whether the given equation represents a circle or not; b) if so, find its center and radius; c) find its domain and range.

1. $x^2 + y^2 + 8x - 2y + 13 = 0$

2. $x^2 + y^2 + 8x - 2y + 14 = 0$

3. $x^2 + y^2 + 8x - 2y + 16 = 0$

4. $3x^2 + 3y^2 - 7x + 11y - 11 = 0$

5. The equations in questions 1 through 3 above are all very similar and each results in a circle centered at (-4, 1). For what values of t will the equation $x^2 + y^2 + 8x - 2y + t = 0$ represent a circle?

6. When we solve the equation $x^2 + y^2 + 8x - 2y + 13 = 0$ for y, we obtain
$y = 1 \pm \sqrt{-x^2 - 8x - 12}$.

a) What do these two equations represent?

b) Reconcile your answer to the domain of this relation (question 1) and the value of the discriminant, $-x^2 - 8x - 12$.

Mathematical Background: The *unit circle* is a circle of radius 1 centered at the origin and is modeled algebraically as $x^2 + y^2 = 1$. In general, the equation of a circle of radius r and center (h, k) is given by $(x-h)^2 + (y-k)^2 = r^2$. (Think of a horizontal translation of h units and a vertical translation of k units of the center.) When the equation is not already in this form, the process of completing the square is used to get it in this form so that the center and radius can be determined. For example, the equation $x^2 - 4x + y^2 - 6y = 0$ is a circle of radius $\sqrt{13}$ centered at (2, 3) because $x^2 - 4x + y^2 - 6y = 0$ can be rewritten as $x^2 - 4x + 4 + y^2 - 6y + 9 = 13$ or simply $(x-2)^2 + (y-3)^2 = 13$.

Program syntax: The program centcir(*equation*) returns the center and radius of *equation*. The program calls the program polycoef().

Exploration #6
Solving Triangles

Program syntax: The program triangle() takes no parameters and the following menu appears upon running it:

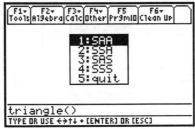

Example 1   In triangle ABC suppose the sides are given as $a = 3.4$, $b = 8.4$, and $c = 6.2$. Find the three angles.

Solution: The triangle has the shape as depicted below. Upon running the program triangle() and choosing option **4:SSS**, we enter the three sides.

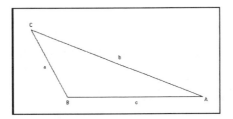

Example 2   Solve the triangle with parts: $a = 6.9$ cm, $b = 9.4$ cm, and $\angle A = 24°$

Solution: This is the SSA case and the reader is urged to try to draw a triangle accurately with these dimensions. We see that two triangles are possible:

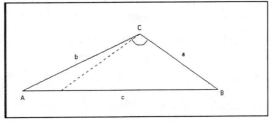

Running the triangle program creates the following screens:

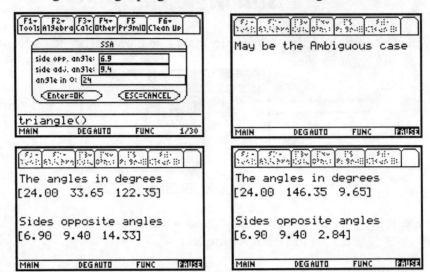

The two possible triangles are listed.

Problems:

1. Two angles of a triangle are known; one is $40°$ and the other is $35°$. If the side opposite the $40°$ angle is 9 cm, solve the triangle.

2. Solve the triangle pictured below:

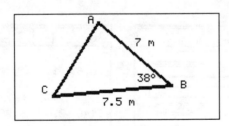

3. Two sides of a triangular garden plot are 10 feet and 16 feet. If the angle between those two sides is 100 degrees, find the length of the third side.

4. A surveyor whose transit is 6 feet from the ground takes a reading on a flagpole 80 feet away. The angle between the sightings to the top and to the bottom is 32 degrees. Find the length of the flagpole.

5. As we mentioned above, it is not always possible to draw a triangle with specified parts. For example, two facts from geometry need to be respected: The sum of the angles of a triangle must equal $180°$ and the measure of any side of a triangle must be less than the sum of the other two sides. Explain why the following cannot be parts of a triangle (in each case assume a, b, and c represent sides and A, B, and C represent angles):

    a) $a = 4.4$ cm, $b = 9.1$ cm and $c = 24.4$ cm.

b) $b = 9$ cm, $c = 5$ cm and $\angle C = 40°$.

6. Show that the area of the shaded portion of the circle in the diagram below is
$$\frac{r^2(\theta - \sin\theta)}{2}$$

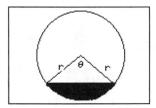

7. In the diagram below, we have parallelogram ABCD. Sides AB and DC are 35 inches long and sides AD and BC are 42 inches long. If angle $\angle ADC = 64°$, determine the length of each diagonal.

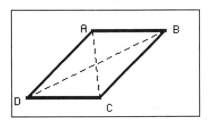

Mathematical Background: By *solving* a triangle we mean that we wish to find all six parts (three angles and three sides) given three parts. There are two laws to use in solving oblique triangles, the Law of Sines and the Law of Cosines.

The law you use depends on the given information – which can be categorized into four cases[5]:

Case	Explanation	Use:
SAA	Two angles and a side	The Law of Sines
SSA	Two sides and an angle opposite one of them	The Law of Sines
SAS	Two sides and an included angle	The Law of Cosines
SSS	Three sides	The Law of Cosines

---

[5] The SSA case is sometimes referred to as the **ambiguous case** because under certain conditions, two different triangles may be possible. Of course, in any case, it may be impossible to construct a triangle with the given information. This is discussed further in the problems.

Exploration #7
Inverse Functions

Example 1   Show that the functions $f(x) = \frac{3-2x}{4}$ and $g(x) = \frac{3-4x}{2}$ are inverses of one another.

Solution: We begin by defining the functions.

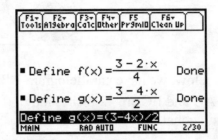

The algebraic test to see if the composition of the two functions yields the identity function is proven below:

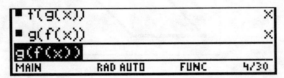

We also can observe the geometric property of inverse functions by graphing f and g along with the line $y = x$. Observe that the graph of $y = f(x)$ is in fact the reflection of $y = g(x)$ about the line $y = x$.

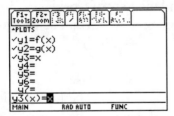   We enter the two functions and the line $y = x$ on the left. On the right, the window values for the graph below.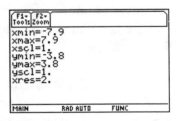

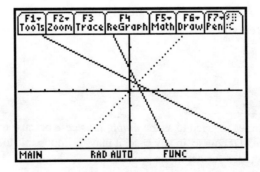

Example 2   Find the inverse of $f(x) = \sqrt{2x-1}$.

Solution: First, notice that the domain of f is $\left\{x \middle| x \geq \frac{1}{2}\right\}$ and the range of f is $\left\{y \middle| y \geq 0\right\}$.

We will allow the CAS to denote the inverse of f with the function name"finv". We use the property of inverse functions – that their composition must be the identity function – to find finv using the solve command. See the screen below:

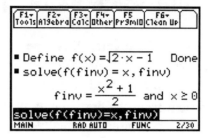

So, $f^{-1}(x) = \frac{x^2+1}{2}$

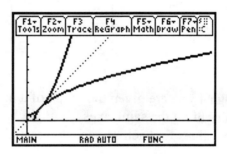

The inverse is entered as $y2(x)$. Notice the use of the "with" command. Y1(x) and y2(x), as before, are graphed in "thick" style; y3 is dot style.

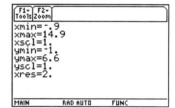

Example 3   The function $y = 4x - \frac{1}{2}x^3$ is *not* a one-to-one function and, therefore, its inverse is not a function. Choose a subset of the points on $y = 4x - \frac{1}{2}x^3$ to insure you have a one-to-one function and graph its inverse.

Solution: The graph of $y = 4x - \frac{1}{2}x^3$ appears below:

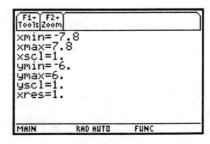
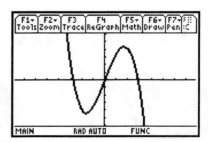

Exploration #7

By tracing, we can see that the x value of the peak is approximately 1.63. So, we place the restriction $x > 1.63$ on the function and it is now one-to-one:

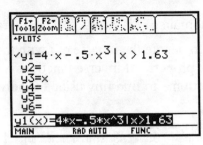 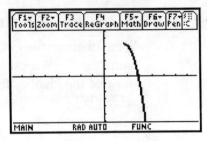

Now, to draw the inverse, this time we will invoke the DrawInv command from the F6 Draw menu. The way this command works is that it simply takes every point (p, q) already graphed and plots its inverse cousin, (q, p). When we choose it from the draw menu, we are temporarily placed in the Home screen and the command actually looks like this:

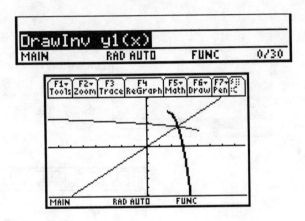

Problems:

In questions 1 through 4 you are given the graph of a one-to-one function. Sketch a graph of the inverse function right on the same axes. It might be helpful first to sketch in the line $y = x$. The window values for each screen capture are the same ones used in Example 3.

1.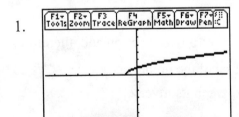

2.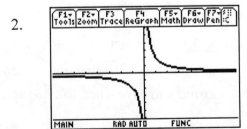

3.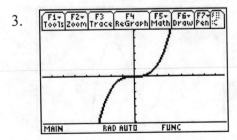

4.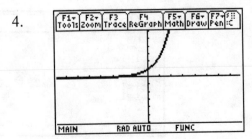

In questions 5 through 10, find the inverse function for each given one-to-one function. Also, state the domain and range of the inverse function.

5. $f(x) = 5x - 7$

6. $f(x) = \sqrt{4 - x^2} \quad 0 \leq x \leq 2$

7. $f(x) = \sqrt[3]{x - 2}$

8. $f(x) = \frac{1}{1+x} \quad x \geq 0$

9. $f(x) = x^{\frac{3}{5}}$

10. $f(x) = (x + 3)^4 \quad x \leq -3$

11.　a) Determine the intersection of the graphs $y = f(x)$ and $y = f^{-1}(x)$ in Example 1.

　　c) In general, if the graphs of $y = f(x)$ and $y = f^{-1}(x)$ intersect, where must the point(s) of intersection be?

Mathematical Background: This exploration examines several examples of functions and finding their inverses. The inverse of a function f is denoted by f^{-1} and has the property that the composition of the inverse with the function yields the identity function. In symbols, $(f^{-1} \circ f)(x) = (f \circ f^{-1})(x) = x$.

1.　Geometrically speaking, two functions are inverses of each other if the graph of one of the functions is the reflection of the other's graph about the line $y = x$.

2.　If the point (4, 3) is a point on the graph of $y = f(x)$, then the point (3, 4) must be a point on the graph of its inverse, f^{-1}

3.　In order for the inverse of $y = f(x)$ to be a function, f must be a *one-to-one* function.

4.　The domain of a function is the range of its inverse and vice versa.

Program syntax: This exploration does not use a program but incorporates the "Define" and "solve(" commands extensively. .

Exploration #8
Animating Trigonometric Functions: Part 1

This exploration uses the program cycshow() which takes no parameters. It creates a dialog box of four menu items. Included in the collection of files that accompany this book are five picture files that can be animated with cycshow.

Example 1 Run the animation on the series called "am" (for amplitude modulation) to see the effect of changing the values of a in $y = a\sin(x)$.

Solution: We begin by choosing the option "2:show animation" since the picture files already exist.

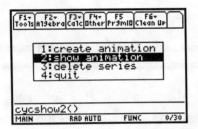

Left: Choose option 2.

Right: User is prompted for the number of views (there are five) and the name of the pictures, "am".

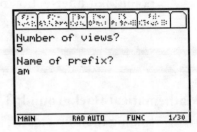

It is not possible to animate on these pages but we depict the five views-- $y = a\sin(x)$ -- where a takes on the values from 1 to 5.

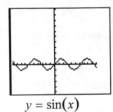 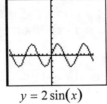 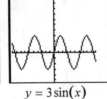 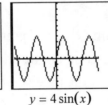 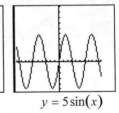

| $y = \sin(x)$ | $y = 2\sin(x)$ | $y = 3\sin(x)$ | $y = 4\sin(x)$ | $y = 5\sin(x)$ |

Example 2 Create an animation of $y = a\cos(x)$ -- where a takes on the values from 1 to 5 to show amplitude modulation of the cosine curve.

Solution: We choose the option "1:create animation" to begin.

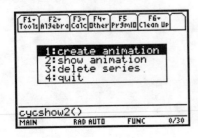

Left: Choose option #1.

Right: We will have five views and they will be named cosam1.pic through cosam5.pic.

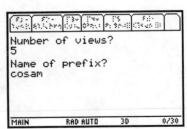

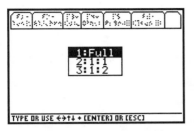 Left: You may choose a full screen picture or a split screen. (On the TI-89, only a 1:1 split is possible.)

Right: You may choose the type of graph screen; for our example, "function" is the appropriate choice.

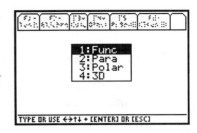

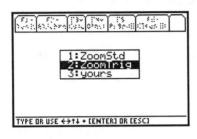 Left: Choose a zoom window or create your own.

Right: Enter the function using i for the screen counter and x for the independent variable.

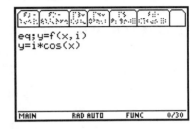

Finally, you can run the "2:show animation" option from the program. Since we cannot depict the animation, below is a figure that overlaps all five of the created cosine curves.

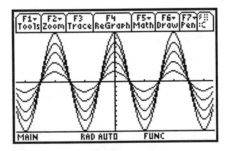

Problems:

1. Example one showed how we can run the "am" (for amplitude modulation) series of pictures to see the effect of a changing amplitude. Also included in your files is an "fm" series of pictures (for frequency modulation). Run that series and observe the effect.

2. a) Graph $y = 3\cos(k \cdot x)$ and observe that the period is $\dfrac{2\pi}{k}$ for and $k > 0$.

   b) Use the program cycshow() to create four period variations of the cosine curve. That is, create $y = 3\cos(i \cdot x)$ where $i = 1, 1.5, 2, 2.5$.

3. See the effect of a negative multiplier by creating an animation of the following:
   $(-1)^k \cdot k \cdot \cos(x)$ for $k = 1, 2, 3, 4$.

4. Show graphically that $\sin(-x) = -\sin(x)$.

5. Show graphically that $\cos(-x) = \cos(x)$

6. a) Why is it more difficult to observe changes in the graph of $y = k \cdot \tan(x)$ for different values of k?

   b) What is the amplitude of the tangent curve?

Mathematical Background: This exploration and the next examine the sine and cosine functions. In general, the function $y = a\sin(bx)$ has **amplitude** $|a|$ and **period** $\frac{2\pi}{b}$.

The amplitude is the greatest value the curve achieves and the period is the length on the horizontal axis required for one complete cycle of the curve.

Program syntax: This exploration uses the program cycshow() which takes no parameters. The program calls another program called animate() and accesses database called gobclear. Cycshow() will allow the user to create a collection of picture files and then animate them, show an already existing collection, or delete a collection (picture files take up a lot of memory).

Exploration #9
Animating Trigonometric Functions: Part 2

<u>Example 1</u>   Let's examine phase shift. Use cycshow() to create a series of four pictures that will animate shift for $y = 2\cos\left(3x + \dfrac{k\pi}{4}\right)$ where $k = 0,1,2,3$.

Solution: This time we choose the first option, "1:create animation". The screen on the left below shows that we must decide on the number of views and the prefix name of the picture files. We chose the name *coshift*.[6] The program also allows us to determine the size of the animation screen (we chose a 1:1 split screen), the graph type (we chose function, of course), and the window values (we chose ZoomTrig).

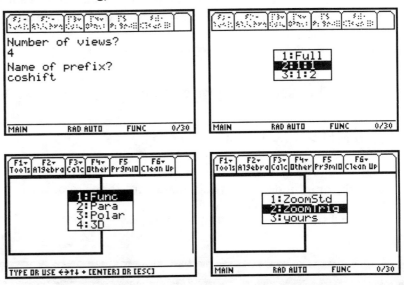

Next, we must be careful because the program uses *i* as the counter. So, the function series is entered as $y = 2\cos\left(3x + \dfrac{(i-1)\pi}{4}\right)$

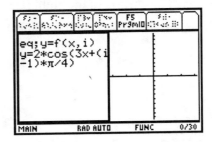

---

[6] Some names are reserved names and cannot be used. For example, y, z, r, u, ui, xt, yt, yi, and c are names we have found that cannot be used.

Now, we are ready to run the animation. We depict the screens below. Notice that the curves shifts to the left an additional $\dfrac{\pi}{12}$ units for each screen:

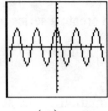
$y = 2\cos(3x)$

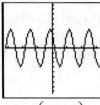
$y = 2\cos\left(3x + \dfrac{\pi}{4}\right)$

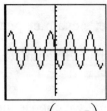
$y = 2\cos\left(3x + \dfrac{\pi}{2}\right)$

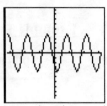
$y = 2\cos\left(3x + \dfrac{3\pi}{4}\right)$

Problems:

1. In this exercise, we will show that the cosine function is a shifted sine function. First of all, from geometry, recall that "co-functions of complementary angles[7] are equal". In symbols for sine and cosine we can write $\cos(x) = \sin\left(\dfrac{\pi}{2} - x\right)$. Now we rewrite $\sin\left(\dfrac{\pi}{2} - x\right)$ as $\sin\left(-x + \dfrac{\pi}{2}\right)$ which, by exercise 3 above, is $-\sin\left(x - \dfrac{\pi}{2}\right)$. Substantiate all this graphically by graphing $y = \cos(x)$, $y = \sin\left(\dfrac{\pi}{2} - x\right)$, and $y = -\sin\left(x - \dfrac{\pi}{2}\right)$.

2. State the amplitude, period and phase shift for each of the following:

   a) $y = 4\sin\left(2x - \dfrac{\pi}{4}\right)$ b) $y = -3\cos\left(2x - \dfrac{\pi}{12}\right)$ c) $y = 2\cos\left(\pi x - \dfrac{\pi}{3}\right)$

Mathematical Background: The graph of $y = a\sin(bx + c)$ has a ***phase shift*** of $-\dfrac{c}{b}$. That means that the graph of $y = a\sin(bx + c)$ is the graph of $y = a\sin(bx)$ horizontally shifted $-\dfrac{c}{b}$ units. The shift is to the right if $-\dfrac{c}{b}$ is positive and to the left if $-\dfrac{c}{b}$ is negative. The cosine function exhibits phase shift similarly.

---

[7] Complementary angles are angles that add up to 90 degrees or $\dfrac{\pi}{2}$ radians.

Exploration #10
Newton's Law of Cooling

Example 1 Take temperatures of a cup of hot coffee at 30 second intervals for six minutes. If you'd prefer, use the data in the file *newtcool* which was created by students actually collecting the data. Also, make note of the room temperature. For the data in *newtcool,* the room temperature was 20.5° C. That data is displayed below:

Time (in minutes)	Temp (degrees C)
0	96
.5	94
1	92
1.5	90
2	88.5
2.5	87
3	85.5
3.5	84
4	83
4.5	81.5
5	80.5
5.5	79
6	78

Newton's Law of Cooling formula is $T = ce^{kt} + T_a$ where T is the temperature of the coffee at any time t and T_a is the room temperature (or *ambient temperature*). Determine the values of c and k in $T = ce^{kt} + T_a$.

Solution: When $t = 0, T = 96$ and we have $96 = ce^{k \cdot 0} + 20.5$ so $c = 75.5$. To find the value of k, use a particular data point, say (6, 78):
$$T = 75.5e^{kt} + 20.5$$
$$78 - 20.5 = 75.5e^{6k}$$

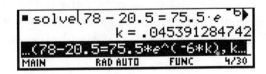

and we see that $k \approx -0.0453913$

Example 2 Plot the graph $T = 75.5e^{-0.0453913t} + 20.5$ along with a scatter plot of the data. Is the theoretical model (Newton's law of cooling) consistent with the experimental data? What is the horizontal asymptote and what is its significant to the physics of the experiment?

Solution: The scatter plot falls right on the theoretical line, $T = 75.5e^{-0.0453913t} + 20.5$ and we conclude that the data is very consistent with the model.

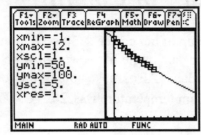 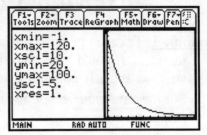

The graph on the right shows that eventually, the coffee's temperature will approach 20.5°C, the temperature of its surroundings! (But it takes almost two hours to get "close".)

Problems.

1. a) Take a cup of hot water to boiling and take measurements as suggested above, at every 30 seconds, for a total of about five or six minutes. Repeat the calculations of Example 1 and the plots of Example2.

    b) Repeat the experiment but this time use a different vessel. (If you used a ceramic cup in part a), use styrofoam here or vice versa.)

    c) What effect does a different cup have on the algebraic model? Is affected?

2. What aspect of the experiment affects c in the equation?

3. Solve (by hand) for t: $T = 75.5e^{kt} + 20.5$.

4. Solve (by hand) for t: $T = ce^{kt} + T_a$.

Mathematical Background: Given a cup of hot coffee, Newton's Law of Cooling states that the rate at which the coffee cools is proportional to the difference in the temperature between the coffee and the room temperature (or *ambient temperature*, T_a). In calculus we can show that this relationship is given by the formula:

$$T = ce^{kt} + T_a$$

where T is the temperature of the coffee at any time t and T_a is the temperature of the coffee's surroundings (that is, room temperature). The values of c and k are constants that are affected by viscosity and ingredients in the coffee, the type of container, and the initial temperature of the coffee.

Program Syntax: There is not a program necessary for this exploration; readers are encouraged to actually collect data and work with that data. A data set called newtcool of times and temperatures is included for convenience.

Exploration #11
The Nature of Polynomial Zeros: Part 1

Example 1   Given that $f(x) = 5x^3 - 35x^2 + 60x$, use the program polyzero() to find $f(1)$ and $f(\frac{7}{2})$. What does this information tell you about zero(s) of *f*?

Solution: We seldom jump into a question like this without using a graph of $y = f(x)$ as visual assistance:

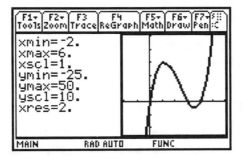

An immediate observation is that since $y = f(x)$ has three *x*-intercepts, then the polynomial $f(x) = 5x^3 - 35x^2 + 60x$ has three real zeros. Now, we use the program polyzero() to find $f(1)$. The program prompts us for the function and the value of *k* (which is 1) as we see below:

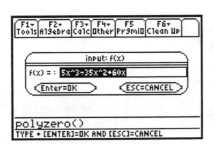 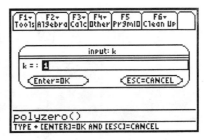

The following output is obtained:

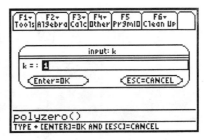

Interpretation: When $f(x) = 5x^3 - 35x^2 + 60x$ is divided by $x - 1$ the quotient is $5x^2 - 30x + 30$ and the remainder is 30. In other words, $f(1) = 30$.

Similarly, when we use the program[8] to find $f\left(\frac{7}{2}\right)$, we see that $f\left(\frac{7}{2}\right) = -\frac{35}{8}$.

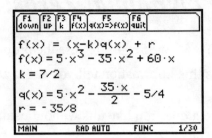

We interpret this screen as $f\left(\frac{7}{2}\right) = -\frac{35}{8}$ and we conclude (because the polynomial goes from being positive to being negative from left to right) that there ***must*** be a zero between $x = 1$ and $x = \frac{7}{2}$

Example 2   Find all the real zeros of $f(x) = x^4 - 3x^3 + 3x - 1$ using the program polyzero().

Solution: The graph of $y = f(x)$ appears below.

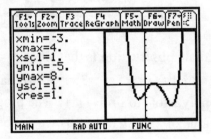

The Rational Roots Theorem states that if a rational root exists, it must be either 1 or –1. We first try $x = -1$ in polyzero().

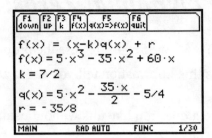

Yes, indeed $x = -1$ is a zero. Now, we proceed to find zeros of $x^3 - 4x^2 + 4x - 1$. (WHY?) The program is very helpful here, simply choose [F5] to place $q(x)$ in place of $f(x)$. Again, the candidates for rational numbers are 1 and -1

The screen on the right below shows that $x = 1$ is a second zero. Since the remaining quotient is a quadratic, we can apply the quadratic formula to find

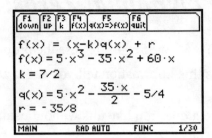

---

[8] To use the same function but alter the value of k, simply choose [F3] and enter 7/2. You **must** enter the number as the exact value 7/2; entering 3.5 will not work.

the final two zeros, $x = \dfrac{3 \pm \sqrt{5}}{2}$. In summary, the four zeros are

$$x = 1, \; x = -1, \; x = \frac{3 + \sqrt{5}}{2}, \text{ and } x = \frac{3 - \sqrt{5}}{2}$$

■

Problems:

1. The reader may be wondering why we spend time discussing the nature of zeros of a polynomial since we have the power of a CAS and its *solve(* and *zeros(* commands. One reason is that neither of those commands addresses multiple roots. Consider the polynomial $f(x) = x^4 - 4x^3 + 16x - 16$.

    a) What is the set of all possible rational zeros for $f(x)$?

    b) Find all the zeros and their multiplicity.

In questions 2 through 8, find all the zeros of the given polynomial, if possible.

2. $f(x) = 2x^3 - 3x^2 - 18x - 8$

3. $f(x) = x^4 - 7x^3 + 3x^2 + 63x - 108$

4. $f(x) = x^4 - 2x^3 - 29x^2 + 10x + 120$

5. $f(x) = x^4 + 2x^3 - 29x^2 - 10x + 120$

6. $f(x) = x^3 - 6x - 4$

7. $f(x) = 10x^3 - 60x - 40$

8. $f(x) = x^4 - 6x^2 - 4x$

9. Consider the graph of a cubic polynomial function $y = f(x)$ below:

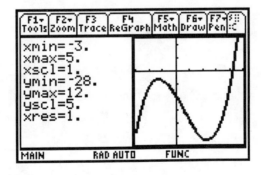

    a) How many real zeros does $f(x)$ have?
    b) How many real zeros does the cubic polynomial $f(x) + 5$ have?
    c) Is there a value of c such that the cubic polynomial $f(x) + c$ has no real zeros?

10. Show that the polynomial $f(x) = x^4 - 7x^2 + 10$ has four real zeros but none of them is rational.

11. Show that the polynomial $f(x) = x^4 - x^3 - 3x^2 + 2x + 2$ has four real zeros but none of them is rational.

Mathematical Background: The ***Fundamental Theorem of Algebra*** states that a polynomial of degree $n \geq 1$ with real coefficients[9] will have exactly n (complex) zeros. Finding these zeros is the topic of this and the next exploration.

Among the tools that are typically used in a precalculus course are Descartes' Rule of Signs, the Remainder Theorem, the Factor Theorem, the Rational Roots Theorem and synthetic division. We will not need Descartes' Rule of Signs or synthetic division for our work here but the reader is encouraged to know these important blocks upon which we build. We state the Remainder Theorem, the Factor Theorem, and the Rational Roots Theorem for easy reference:

   Remainder Theorem: If a polynomial $f(x)$ is divided by $x - k$, then the remainder is $f(k)$.

   Factor Theorem: A polynomial $f(x)$ has a factor $x - k$ if and only if $f(k) = 0$.

   Rational Roots Theorem: If a polynomial $f(x) = a_n x^n + a_{n-1} x^{n-1} + \cdots + a_1 x + a_0$ has integer coefficients and if the rational number $\frac{p}{q}$ is a zero of $f(x)$ (with p and q having no common factors), then p is a factor of a_0 and q is a factor of a_n.

Program syntax: The program polyzero() takes no parameters and allows the user to input a polynomial $f(x)$ and a value of k.

---

[9] All polynomials investigated in this book will be assumed to have real coefficients.

Exploration #12

The Nature of Polynomial Zeros: Part 2

<u>Example 1</u> Find all the zeros of $f(x) = x^4 - 5x^3 + 9x^2 - 8x + 4$.

Solution: A fourth degree polynomial has four complex zeros but the CAS command "cZeros(" only yields three of them. (This is the multiplicity of zeros addressed in problem one of the previous exploration.)

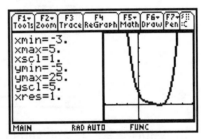

We will first look for rational zeros and the set of all possible rational roots is $\{\pm 1, \ \pm 2, \ \pm 4\}$ and the graph below[10] helps us eliminate all rational numbers in the list except $x = 2$.

Now, employing polyzero with $k = 2$ yields the following output:

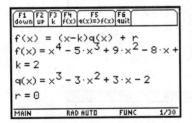

After observing that 2 is a zero ($r=0$) we press the [F5] key to now work with $x^3 - 3x^2 + 3x - 2$. On the right, we see that 2 is a root of multiplicity two. Once down to the quadratic, $x^2 - x + 1$ we can use the quadratic formula for the two complex roots.

Finally, the four zeros are $x = 2$, $x = 2$, $x = \frac{1}{2} - \frac{\sqrt{3}}{2}i$, $x = \frac{1}{2} + \frac{\sqrt{3}}{2}i$. Observe that the complex numbers are a conjugate pair. Also, the original polynomial, $f(x) = x^4 - 5x^3 + 9x^2 - 8x + 4$, can be factored over the real numbers as

---

[10] Actually, Descartes' Rule of Signs tells us that there can be no negative real zero to this polynomial.

$(x-2)^2(x^2-x+1)$ or over the complex numbers it factors as

$$(x-2)^2\left(x-\frac{1}{2}+\frac{\sqrt{3}}{2}i\right)\left(x-\frac{1}{2}-\frac{\sqrt{3}}{2}i\right)$$

■

Example 2   Find all the real zeros of $f(x)=2x^3-5x^2+7x-6$ using the program polyzero().

Solution: Since $f(x)$ is an odd degree polynomial, it must have at least one real zero. The set of all possible rational roots is $\left\{\pm1,\ \pm\frac{1}{2},\ \pm2,\ \pm3,\ \pm\frac{3}{2},\ \pm6\right\}$ but again by Descartes' Rule of Signs, the negative values can be eliminated. A graph of $y=f(x)$ appears below.

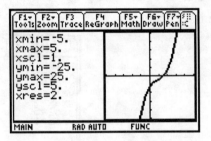

We try the value $k=\frac{3}{2}$ in polyzero() and observe that it is, in fact, a zero of the polynomial since the remainder is zero. See the output below:

```
F1    F2 F3 F4      F5       F6
down  UP  k  f(x) q(x)=>f(x) quit

f(x) = (x-k)q(x) + r
f(x) = 2·x³ - 5·x² + 7·x - 6
k = 3/2
q(x) = 2·x² - 2·x + 4
r = 0

MAIN      RAD AUTO   FUNC    21/30
```

Thus, we can say that the polynomial $f(x)=2x^3-5x^2+7x-6$ is factorable as $\left(x-\frac{3}{2}\right)(2x^2-2x+4)$. However, we prefer to write that factored product as $(2x-3)(x^2-x+2)$. The quadratic factor, x^2-x+2 has as its two zeros $\frac{1}{2}+\frac{\sqrt{7}}{2}i$ and $\frac{1}{2}-\frac{\sqrt{7}}{2}i$ and the three zeros have been found.

■

Problems:

1. There are three cube roots of 8. Find all three by finding the zeros of the polynomial
    $$f(x) = x^3 - 8$$

2. There are four fourth roots of 16. Find all four by finding the zeros of the polynomial
    $$f(x) = x^4 - 16.$$

3. (True or False) Every odd degree polynomial (with real coefficients) must have at least one real zero.

4. (True or False) Every even degree polynomial (with real coefficients) must have at least one real zero.

5. Solve (find all three solutions) $2x^3 + 3x^2 - 6x - 9 = 0$

6. Solve (find all five solutions) $x^5 - 3x^4 + 5x^3 - 7x^2 + 6x - 2 = 0$

7. a) Find a third degree polynomial that has, among its three zeros, the numbers 1 and $1 - 2i$.
    b) Explain why the answer to part a) is not unique. Can you generalize your answer to part a)?

8. a) How many real zeros does the polynomial $f(x) = x^3 - 4x - 2$ have?
    b) How many *rational* zeros does the polynomial have?

Mathematical Background: This is a continuation of the previous exploration. Here, when we refer to *polynomial*, we mean an expression of the form
$$f(x) = a_n x^n + a_{n-1} x^{n-1} + \cdots + a_1 x + a_0.$$
This is a polynomial of degree n and, as before, we assume all the coefficients, a_i, are real numbers. Such a polynomial, according to the **Fundamental Theorem of Algebra**, has n complex zeros with non-real complex numbers appearing in complex conjugate pairs.

Program syntax: Again, we will use the program polyzero() which takes no parameters and allows the user to input a polynomial $f(x)$ and a value of k.

Exploration #13
Sequences and Progressions

Example 1. An arithmetic progression.   Mary accepts a job as a reporter with a starting salary of $21,000 for the first year and an increase of $1800 per year thereafter. What will her salary be for the eighth year and what will her total earnings be for the first eight years?

Solution: The sequence can be generated on the home screen by entering
seq(21000+(n-1)*1800,n,1,8) and the output is:
    {21000, 22800, 24600, 26400, 28200, 30000, 31800, 33600} so we can see that Mary's salary in the eighth year is $33,600.

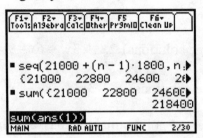

We sum the sequence of eight terms to see that her accumulated salary is $218,400. Finally, we mention that this could be accomplished within the program sequence() as well. The program also supplies a plot of the sequence.

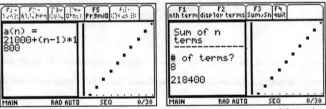

Left: We enter the sequence function and observe a plot. Any arithmetic progression will have a linear plot. Right: Choose F3 to find the sum of a sequence.

Example 2. A geometric progression.   Marla takes a job offering a starting salary of $21,000 with an increase of 5% per year, based on the previous year's salary. Determine her salary for the ninth year and determine the total amount of earnings for the first nine years.

Solution: An increase of 5% per year means that the common ratio in this geometric progression is 1.05. The sequence function is $a_n = 21000 \cdot (1.05)^{n-1}$ and we use the program's F2 option for displaying terms, four at a time. See below.

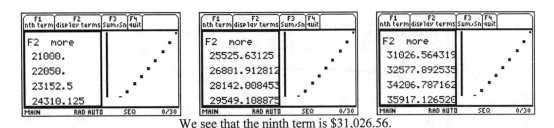

We see that the ninth term is \$31,026.56.

The sum of the first nine terms is \$231,557.85 as we see in the screen below:

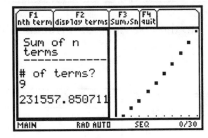

The next two examples involve sequences that are neither arithmetic nor geometric.

Example 3   Consider the sequence $a_n = 1, \dfrac{1}{4}, \dfrac{1}{9}, \cdots, \dfrac{1}{n^2}$ as well as its *sequence*

of partial sums, $\displaystyle\sum_{k=1}^{n} \dfrac{1}{k^2}$. What does each approach as n approaches infinity?

Solution: We choose to examine these sequences directly, without the use of the
program sequence(). First, we set the mode setting for graphs to
"4:Sequence". We enter the sequence as $u1(n)$ with an initial value (denoted
on the Y= editor as $ui1$) of 1. The sequence of partial sums is entered as
$u2(n)$:

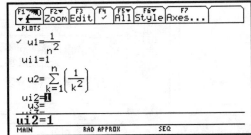

Left: We enter the sequence $u1$ and $u2$ as well as their initial values. Right: We choose window
parameters. Notice that there will be 75 terms calculated and plotted (nmax=75).

We have chosen the "square" style for $u1$ and "thick" style for $u2$. The graph
is observed below.

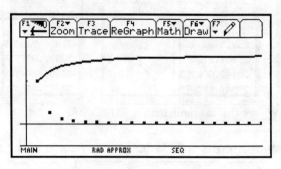

The value of the partial sums appears to approach 1.6

$u1(n)$ is approaching 0 as n gets large.

If we trace[11] to the last value of n (recall, nmax=75), we can see that

$$\sum_{k=1}^{75} \frac{1}{k^2} \approx 1.631689$$

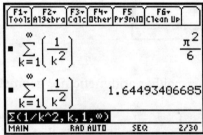
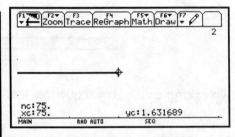

The *exact* value of the infinite sequence of partial sums can also be obtained.

Example 4. A sequence defined recursively.

To be defined *recursively* means to be defined in terms of itself. What happens if you repeatedly take the cosine of the cosine of the cosine (etc) of an angle? Does this value converge on a particular number regardless of the original angle?

Solution: We enter $u1(n) = \cos\big(u1(n-1)\big)$ -- that is, to find any particular term, you take the cosine of the preceding term. See the screens below:

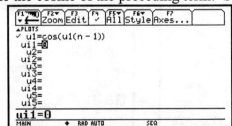

Under F7 Axes, we choose to make this a 1:Time plot.

---

[11] After pressing F3 to trace, simply press 75 to reach the end.

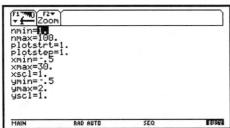 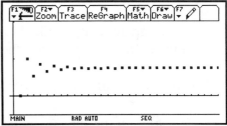

The plot indicates that the terms of the sequence appear to be approaching a particular value.

Next, we trace the 100th term and see that its value is approximately 0.739085 as witnessed in the screen below:

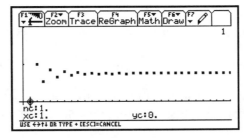 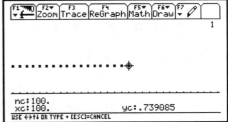

A very interesting variation of a sequence plot is web plot. A web plot graphs the sequence by using $u1(n)$ values for the vertical axis and $u1(n-1)$ values for the horizontal axis. If a sequence converges to one specific value, as we have in our example, the web plot should converge to that point. The visual effect is very interesting.

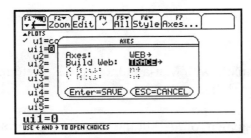 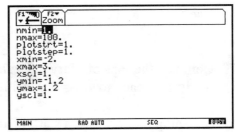

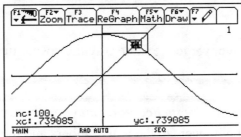

The web is constructed as you trace by repeated pressing the right cursor key.

Problems:

1. Find the fifteenth term and the sum of the first fifteen terms for the sequence below:

$$3,-1,-5,-9\cdots=\left\{3+(n-1)(-4)\right\}$$

2. A taxi company charges \$3.00 for the first 1/8 of a mile and 25 cents for every 1/8 of a mile thereafter. How much is the fare for a 15-mile ride?

3. The population of a small city is 20,000 and is increasing by 2.5% each year.

      a) If the annual population of this city is thought of as a sequence, is that sequence a geometric progression, an arithmetic progression or neither?

      b) What will the population be in 20 years, assuming the same growth rate of 2.5%?

      c) How long will it take for the population to double?

4. The term "**series**" refers to a summation of terms in a sequence. A special infinite series, the **harmonic series**, is $\sum_{k=1}^{\infty}\dfrac{1}{k}$. It can be shown in higher mathematics that this infinite series does not converge to a value, rather it becomes infinitely large. That is difficult to see by looking at the sequence of partial sums. Compute the sum of the first 1000 terms.

5. Consider the repeating decimal expansion: 0.424242…. This can be thought of as a sum of the sequence: $.42,.0042,.000042,.00000042\cdots=\left\{.42\cdot(.01)^{(n-1)}\right\}$. Using the formula $S=\dfrac{a_1}{1-r}$ for this infinite sum, express the repeating decimal as a fraction.

6. Use the method of Exercise 5 to show that the decimal expansion 0.99999… is **exactly** equal to 1.

7. Compare the jobs of Mary in Example 1 with Marla in Example 2. Determine how long it will take each to gross one million dollars at her job.

8. In example 4, we used a starting argument of $ui1$ but the recursive cosine series converges for **any** initial value! Regraph the sequence plot using various other values of $ui1$.

9. Does the sine function converge the same way the cosine function does in Example 4?

Mathematical Background: A *sequence function* (usually denoted a_n as opposed to $a(n)$) maps a subset of the integers to the real numbers and the collection of range elements of this function is usually referred to as a *sequence*. A sequence may be finite or infinite. It may converge (to a particular real number) or it may not.

Two special sequences often studied at this level are **arithmetic sequences** (or *arithmetic progressions*) and **geometric sequences** (or *geometric progressions*). An arithmetic progression has the property that each term differs from the next by the same constant, called the ***common difference***.

Two formulas associated with arithmetic progressions are $a_n = a_1 + (n-1)d$ and

$S_n = \dfrac{n}{2}(a_1 + a_n)$ where a_1 is the first term in the sequence, a_n is the nth term of the

sequence, d is the common difference, and S_n is the sum of the first n terms.

A geometric progression has the property that the ratio of a term to its preceding term is a constant, called the ***common ratio*** (usually denoted as r). The formulas associated

with geometric progressions are $a_n = a_1 \cdot r^{n-1}$ and $S_n = \dfrac{a_1(1-r^n)}{1-r}$. If $|r| < 1$, the latter

formula becomes $S = \dfrac{a_1}{1-r}$.

Program syntax: This exploration uses the program sequence() which takes no parameters and is used to help facilitate the entering and graphing of sequences.

Exploration #14

Systems of Linear Equations

In an earlier exploration, we examined systems of two equations in two variables. Here we will study systems of linear equations involving at least three variables.

Example 1   Solve the following system of equations:

$$x - y + 6z = 8$$
$$3x - y - 2z = 6$$
$$2x - 3y + 4z = 16$$

Solution: The way we will choose to solve this system is by means of **row reduction**. In particular, the "rref" command will produce the reduced row echelon form of the 3-by-4 matrix representing the system.

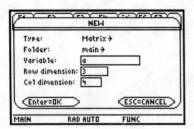   Left: From the APPS key, choose 6:Data/Matrix editor. We named our matrix *a;* it is a 3-by-4 matrix.

Right: The matrix *a* is entered.

The reduced row echelon form is displayed below:

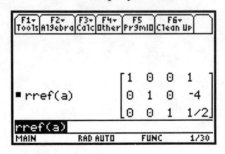

Interpretation: $x = 1$, $y = -4$, and $z = 1/2$

Example 2   Solve the system of equations:

$$x_1 + x_2 + x_3 = 4$$
$$2x_1 - x_2 + x_3 = 0$$
$$4x_1 + x_2 + 3x_3 = 8$$

Solution: We enter the 3-by-4 matrix and call it *b*. Then we row-reduce it to its reduced row echelon form to obtain:

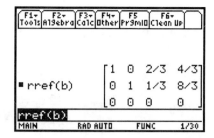

Interpretation: There is not a unique solution to this system; it is a ***dependent system***. We can however, solve for two of the variables in terms of the third. In this case, we choose x_1 and x_2 as our basic variables and solve for them in terms of x_3:

$$x_1 + \frac{2}{3}x_3 = \frac{4}{3} \qquad x_1 = \frac{4}{3} - \frac{2}{3}x_3$$
$$\text{or}$$
$$x_2 + \frac{1}{3}x_3 = \frac{8}{3} \qquad x_2 = \frac{8}{3} - \frac{1}{3}x_3$$

Would you like practice in solving consistent, independent systems of linear equations? We provide you with a program called linear(). It will create a system of equations from the solutions you provide. For example, suppose you want to create a system of three equations in the three variables x, y, and z having solutions

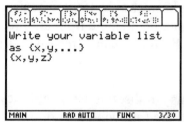

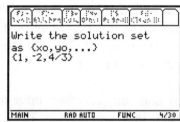

The system is output below. Be aware that the system you obtain will probably be

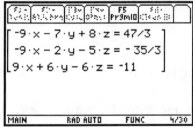

different since the program uses a random number generator for some of its work. Of course, a system created around a given solution should not be expected to be unique!

Problems:

1. Solve the 4-by-4 system given below:
$$x_1 + x_2 + x_3 + x_4 = 3$$
$$x_1 - x_2 = -3$$
$$3x_1 + x_3 + 2x_4 = 2$$
$$x_2 + x_3 + 6x_4 = 31$$

2. Instead of solving two separate 3-by-3 systems for the systems listed below, show that by reducing one 3-by-5 matrix, the two sets of solutions can be found.
$$x_1 - x_2 + x_3 = 7 \qquad x_1 - x_2 + x_3 = 3$$
$$2x_1 + 3x_2 - x_3 = 4 \text{ and } 2x_1 + 3x_2 - x_3 = 13$$
$$3x_1 + 6x_2 - 4x_3 = 3 \qquad 3x_1 + 6x_2 - 4x_3 = 20$$

3. The system $\begin{array}{l} x_1 + x_2 + x_3 = 4 \\ 2x_1 - x_2 + x_3 = 0 \\ 4x_1 + x_2 + 3x_3 = 9 \end{array}$ is an **inconsistent system**. What is the indicator in the reduced row echelon form that there can be no solution to this system?

4. Katie has $35,000 that has been divided into three investments. Part of the money is invested in a savings account with an annual rate of 6% interest, part in 7% annual-yield bonds, and the remainder is invested in a business. In 1999, when she lost 6% of the money that she invested in the business, her net income from all three investments was $660. If she invested $3000 more in the business than in the savings account, how much was invested in each?

5. A toy company produces three main items – dolls, train sets, and tricycles. In the months of June, July, and August, 1999 they sold the following quantities:

	Dolls	Train sets	Tricycles	Income
June	10	6	40	$20,300
July	4	5	100	$46,570
August	15	20	200	$96,200

Determine the selling price for each of the three toys.

6. Repeat exercise 4 for the following information:

	Dolls	Train sets	Tricycles	Income
September	10	6	40	$20,300
October	4	5	100	$46,570
November	14	11	140	$66,870

7. a) Run the program linear() for the solution $x = 2$, $y = -4$, and $z = 6$.
    b) Repeat part a). How do you reconcile that the two systems output are not the same?

Mathematical Background: A system of m equations in n variables is of the form:

$$a_{11}x_1 + a_{12}x_2 + \cdots + a_{1n}x_n = b_1$$
$$a_{21}x_1 + a_{22}x_2 + \cdots + a_{2n}x_n = b_2$$
$$\vdots$$
$$a_{m1}x_1 + a_{m2}x_2 + \cdots + a_{mn}x_n = b_m$$

We can solve this system by performing row operations on the m-by-$n+1$ matrix,

$$\begin{bmatrix} a_{11} & a_{12} & \cdots & a_{1n} & b_1 \\ a_{21} & a_{22} & \cdots & a_{2n} & b_2 \\ \vdots & & & & \\ a_{m1} & a_{m2} & \cdots & a_{mn} & b_m \end{bmatrix}$$ until the matrix is in reduced row echelon form.

If one or more rows of the reduced row echelon form contains all zeros, the system is said to be *dependent* and infinitely many solutions may occur. On the other hand, if a row is composed of zeros except for the rightmost entry, the system is said to be *inconsistent* and no solutions occur.

Program syntax: To create a (square) consistent, independent system of n linear equations in n variables we use the program linear(). It takes no parameters.

Exploration #15
Polar Graphs

Example 1.   Graph $r = 1 - 2\cos\theta$.

Solution: We begin by first placing the CAS in polar form as shown in the screen
below:

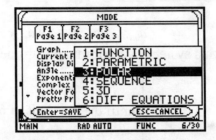

Observe that now, the "Y=" editor becomes the "$r =$" editor and that the
independent variable is θ. The graph, called a *limaçon*, is pictured below;
variations of it are discussed in the exercises.

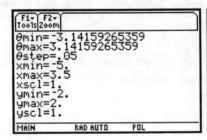 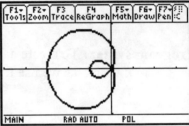

Example 2.   Graph $r = 2\sin(5\theta)$.

Solution: The curve, a member of the "rose" curve or "petal" curve is depicted below;
it has five petals. In general, $r = k\sin(n\theta)$ is a rose with n petals if n is odd
and it has $2n$ petals if n is even. A similar property holds for $r = k\cos(n\theta)$.

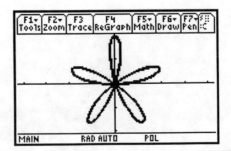

Example 3   Consider the polar function $r = 1 - \sin\theta$. Its graph is a curve that is a member of the family of curves called *cardioids*. Graph it.

Solution: After performing a "ZoomSqr" command, we have the following window values and graph:

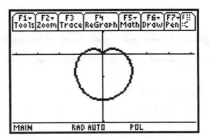

Problems:

1.   Convert each of these rectangular coordinate pairs to polar coordinates.
  a) $(-3, 4)$
  b) $(-8, 15)$

  c) $(-8, -15)$
  d) $(-2.45, 6.91)$

2.   Convert each of these polar coordinate pairs to rectangular coordinates.
  a) $\left(3, \dfrac{3\pi}{2}\right)$
  b) $(2.5, 4.93)$

  c) $(2.5, 11.213)$
  d) $(2.5, -1.353)$

Examine the graphs of each of the polar functions in questions 3 through 6. Can you substantiate the statement about the number of petals and the value of n?

3. $r = 2\cos(3\theta)$
4. $r = 3\sin(5\theta)$

5. $r = 2\sin(2\theta)$
6. $r = 3\cos(4\theta)$

The family of curves called *limaçons* take the form $r = a \pm b\cos(\theta)$ or $r = a \pm b\sin(\theta)$ where $a > 0$ and $b > 0$. Sketch each limaçon in questions 7 and 8.

7.   A limaçon with an inner loop: $r = 1 + 2\sin(\theta)$.

8.   A limaçon with a dimple: $r = 3 + 2\cos(\theta)$.

9.   A graph of the polar function $r = a \cdot \theta$ is called a ***spiral of Archimedes***. Sketch $r = 2\theta$ for $\theta \geq 0$.

10. a) Show that the polar function $r = \dfrac{b}{\sin\theta - m\cos\theta}$ is equivalent to the rectangular

function $y = mx + b$ by substituting $r\cos\theta$ for x and $r\sin\theta$ for y.

b) Graph $r = \dfrac{2}{\sin\theta - 3\cos\theta}$.

Mathematical Background: As we have seen, a point P in the plane has unique Cartesian coordinate system coordinates (x, y). The point can also be labeled in the **polar coordinate system** with (r, θ) where r is the directed distance from the origin to the point P and θ is the directed angle, measured counterclockwise, through P. The polar coordinate representation of a point is *not* unique.

The point, for example, $(3, -4)$ is converted to its polar representation, $(5, 0.9273)$ in the screens below.

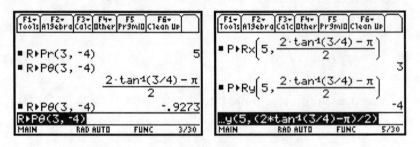

Note that both $(5, 0.9273)$ and $(5, 0.9273 + 2\pi)$ have the same representation when converted to rectangular coordinates, $(3, -4)$.

The relationships among $x, y, r,$ and θ are given by the following four equations:

$$x = r\cos\theta \qquad\qquad y = r\sin\theta$$

$$\tan\theta = \frac{y}{x} \qquad\qquad r^2 = x^2 + y^2$$

In this exploration, we will graph equations of the form $r = f(\theta)$; that is equations where r is expressed as a function of θ.

Program syntax: This exploration does not utilize any programs.

Exploration #16
Linear Programming: The Simplex Method

Example 1   Solve the following linear programming problem:
Maximize $P = 5x + 3y$ subject to:[12]

$$4x + 2y \le 60$$
$$x + y \le 20$$
$$x \ge 0$$
$$y \ge 0$$

Solution: The program lp() will solve this problem; we enter

$$lp\left(5x + 3y, \{4x + 2y \le 60, x + y \le 20\}, \{x, y\}, \text{"max"}\right).$$

In other words, the parameters needed by the program are the optimization expression, the list of constraints, the list of variables, and the string (either "max" or "min"). The program then establishes the *initial tableau* and pivots until a solution is found. The initial tableau is:

x	y	s_2	s_2	
4	2	1	0	60
1	1	0	1	20
-5	-3	0	0	0

The solution occurs when both x and y are 10 and the maximum value of P is 80:

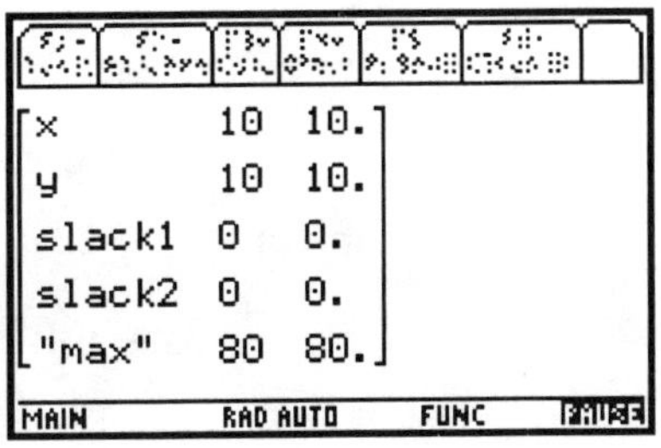

Example 2   Use the program lp() to solve the following linear programming problem: Minimize $Q = 200x_1 + 105x_2 + 90x_3$ subject to:

---

[12] The theory of the Simplex Method includes the notion of *slack* variables. The constraint $4x + 2y \le 60$, for example, is rewritten as $4x + 2y + s_1 = 60$ where s_1 is the positive slack variable that allows the inequality to appear as an equation.

$$2x_1 + x_2 - 10x_3 \geq 8$$
$$x_1 + x_2 + 9x_3 \geq 5$$
$$x_1 \geq 0$$
$$x_2 \geq 0$$
$$x_3 \geq 0$$

Solution:[13] We enter
$$\text{lp}\left(200x1 + 105x2 + 90x3, \{2x1 + x2 - 10x3 \geq 8, x1 + x2 + 9x3 \geq 5\}, \{x1, x2, x3\}, "\text{min}"\right)$$

x1	3	3.
x2	2	2.
x3	0	0.
slack1	0	0.
slack2	0	0.
"min"	810	810.

MAIN   RAD AUTO   FUNC   PAUSE

We see that the minimum value of Q is 810 and occurs when
$x_1 = 3$, $x_2 = 2$, and $x_3 = 0$.

A final note: if the program does not converge, retry the problem a second time but include the trivial constraints this time (i.e., $x \geq 0$, $y \geq 0$, etc.)

Problems:

1. Maximize $P = x + 5y + z$ subject to:

$$3x - y + 2z \leq 24$$
$$x + y + z \leq 22$$
$$x + 2y + 3z \leq 36$$
$$x \geq 0$$
$$y \geq 0$$
$$z \geq 0$$

---

[13] The TI-89 and TI-92PLUS versions of this program allow for vertical and horizontal scrolling of large matrices. For the TI-92, you may want to view the matrix, stored in the variable name ANSWER, in another fashion. Go to the [VAR-LINK] menu, highlight the variable ANSWER.MAT and press [F6] to view its contents.

2. Maximize $P = x_1 + 2x_2 + 10x_3$ subject to:

$$3x_1 + 2x_2 \leq 14$$
$$x_1 + 10x_3 \leq 102$$
$$x_1 + x_2 + 5x_3 \leq 56$$
$$x_2 \leq 4$$
$$x_3 \leq 10$$
$$x_1 \geq 0$$
$$x_2 \geq 0$$
$$x_3 \geq 0$$

3. The Embryo Toy Company manufactures two toys: wooden block sets and wooden trains. Due to limited facilities the company cannot produce more than 40 block sets per week and cannot produce more than 60 trains per week. Furthermore the total number of toys produced cannot exceed 80. The profit for each block set is $2 and the profit for each train set is $3. How many of each toy should the company produce to maximize profit? What is that maximum achievable profit?

4. Minimize: $Q = 2x + 4y$ subject to:

$$2x + y \geq 5$$
$$4x - y \leq -2$$
$$6x \geq 3$$
$$x \geq 0$$
$$y \geq 0$$

5. Suppose the Finite Manufacturing Company produces an item in two factories (Iowa City and Duluth) and ships them to three different distribution centers (Cincinnati, Belleville, and Lexington). Shipping costs are as follows:

> To ship one ton from Iowa City to Cincinnati costs $5
> To ship one ton from Iowa City to Belleville costs $4.
> To ship one ton from Iowa City to Lexington costs $8.
> To ship one ton from Duluth to Cincinnati costs $4.
> To ship one ton from Duluth to Belleville costs $3.
> To ship one ton from Duluth to Lexington costs $6.

Next month, because of demand, Cincinnati needs at least 50 tons, Belleville needs at least 50 tons and Lexington needs 40 tons. If Iowa City has at most 40 tons on hand and Duluth has at most 100 tons, minimize Finite's shipping costs.

Mathematical Background: A *linear programming problem* involves the objective of either maximizing something (profit, for example) or minimizing something (like costs), subject to certain restrictions called *constraints*. These constraints are expressed as linear inequalities and their simultaneous solution forms a convex set of points in the plane. The *simplex method* is a procedure for solving a linear programming problem with matrices. It involves being able to locate the *pivot* and perform row transformations on the matrix (or *tableau*) until all elements in the bottom row are nonnegative.

Program syntax: The program lp() returns the transformed tableaux with both exact and approximate values for all variables (including slack variables). Here, the parameters for the program are the objective function, a list of the constraints, a list of the variables, and the string that is either "max" or "min". The program calls five other programs, apivotf(), bpivotf(), constrs(), and lpsol() as well as the functions polycoef() and pivot().

NOTES

Other Books of Interest

The TI-86/85 Reference Guide by Nelson Rich and Lawrence Gilligan, GILMAR Publishing (Cincinnati, 1997) ISBN 1-888808-01-2.

Diskette of 34 programs to accompany *The TI-86/85 Reference Guide* (above) by Michael B. Schneider, GILMAR (Cincinnati, 1997) ISBN for PC: 1-888808-03-9; for MAC: 1-888808-02-0.

Mastering the TI-92: Explorations from Algebra through Calculus, by Nelson Rich, Judith Rose, and Lawrence Gilligan. GILMAR (Cincinnati, 1996) ISBN 0-9626661-9-x.

The TI-85 Reference Guide by Nelson Rich and Lawrence Gilligan, GILMAR (Cincinnati, 1993) ISBN 0-9626661-6-5.

Applied Calculus, Fourth Edition by Claudia Taylor and Lawrence Gilligan, Brooks/Cole Publishing (Pacific Grove, CA: 1996) ISBN 0-534-33971-9.

Linear Algebra Experiments Using DERIVE® by Mary Salter and Lawrence Gilligan, GILMAR (Cincinnati, 1992) ISBN 0-9626661-4-9.